ARUBA, A BRIEF HI

THE EARLY DAYS OF ARUBA, LAGO ARRIVES,

THE DEVIL'S ISLAND ESCAPEES 1937,

ANTILLA SINKING, AND THE U-156 ATTACK

ED   SONNENBERG-MCGLYNN

TABLE OF CONTENTS

INTRODUCTION 1
OUR ARRIVAL IN THE UNITED STATES 2
A SHORT HISTORY OF ARUBA 6
LIFE IN ARUBA 12
JAN FREDERICK QUAST 14
ISAAC WAGEMAKER 17
THE BACHELORS, THE COPS, AND THE RIOT OF 1929 25
THE DEVIL'S ISLAND ESCAPEES: ARRIVAL IN ARUBA IN 1937 27
GERMANY INVADES THE NETHERLANDS 29
ARUBA AT WAR, MAY 10, 1940 30
THE MEN OF THE U-BOATS 35
WEST INDIES ISLE SHELLED BY SUBMARINES U-156 AND CAPT. HARTENSTEIN ATTACK ARUBA, FEBRUARY 16, 1942. 37
THE ATTACK AS NOTED ONSHORE 38
THE END OF THE U-BOATS 42
THE WRAP-UP 43
ARUBA MISCELLANEOUS--AT THAT TIME 44
A SHORT EXAMPLE OF THE LANGUAGE: 45
A FINAL NOTE 46

INTRODUCTION

ARUBA, THE NETHERLANDS ANTILLES

The following incidents are accurate to the best of my ability. However, I expect that there are mistakes which others will rectify, especially in the area of the sinking of the *Antilla* and the U-156 attack on February 1942.

Some people believe that the *Antilla* carried supplies for the German submarines. I have no reason to believe or to deny the charge. Records state that the ship was carrying sulfur from Texas when it was trapped by the war.

The Antilla, unable to sail home because of the French and British warships which waited for it, sought refuge off the coast of Aruba in the neutral Dutch West Indies. That neutrality ceased on May 10, 1940, when German troops seized the Netherlands and as a result, Aruba was no longer a safe-haven for the ship. From what I recall of the story, the German crew, having no choice, set the ship on fire and scuttled it.

According to the story, a group of ten men armed with ten rifles last fired around 1900, sailed out on a launch to force the German captain to surrender the ship on May 10, 1940. Supposedly, there were only eighty bullets for the rifles. In an alternate version of the story, Dutch marines boarded the ship, took the thirty five crew members ashore by launch and interned them.

Did Lt. Governor Wagemaker of Aruba lead the group of ten that sailed to the *Antilla?* Some stories say that he did.

The ship went down in fifty feet of water not far from the California Lighthouse. When the ship started to sink, imperiling the safety of the marines, they left quickly. As for the German crew members, in another version of the story, they jumped into the sea and swam to the California lighthouse. Because Aruba had no jail for the crew, they camped out, the members disappearing one by one over the following weeks.

At any rate, I have no idea of which version is correct. Confusion and fake news are nothing new in the world. Fake news easily goes back as far as Emperor Augustus of Rome telling the people that he would restore the republic, neglecting to tell the future emperors about the intended restoration.

Fake news goes back even further when the snake tells Eve not to worry about eating the Fruit of the Forbidden Tree.

However, the facts are clear that a group went out to demand the surrender of the ship. Captain Schmidt of the *Antilla* refused to surrender, and he had his crew set the ship afire and scuttle it.

Anyway, our family album has photos of the German crew members camped out in a makeshift shelter at the California lighthouse. The members obviously had a sense of humor because the sign over the hut reads Schloss Heidelburg—Heidelburg Castle.

As for the U-156 attack and pandemonium in the early hours of February 16, 1942, I expect that the records are wildly exaggerated, which is normal under the circumstances.

As for the 1937 Devil's Island escapees who found their way to Aruba, I relied on the news that the escapees reached Colombia, celebrated their freedom, and were turned over to the French authorities on the following morning.

Regarding the original inhabitants of the island, were they the Caribs or the Arawaks? Unfortunately, there are no tribe members around to clear up the matter for us.

OUR ARRIVAL IN THE UNITED STATES

We Sonnenbergs had a heckuva of a problem getting into the USA.

Just before we left the island, someone stole all of our family papers: birth certificates and marriage license. I figure that it was the Germans who needed some nice Dutch papers to sneak a family of spies into the USA to do whatever they could against America.

Luckily, the passports were kept separately, so we were able to sail on the Santa Paula for New York.

Unfortunately, Mom was terribly seasick, so I was left to amuse myself. I amused myself by tossing stuff off the ship.

Early in the war, captains learned quickly not to toss anything overboard because U-boats followed such trails and torpedoed the ships.

The captain confined me to quarters, Mom went out on deck, leaving me alone and really angry. Enjoying my brat-itude stage and not realizing the seriousness of the situation, I thoroughly destroyed the passports with a handy fountain pen which tore the heck out of the papers.

The captain radioed ahead that we, the Sonnenbergs, were arriving without proper entry documents.

As a result, the government did not allow the ship to dock in New York. Instead, Cordell Hull, Secretary of State, and five FBI agents came aboard in the harbor and arrested Mom, charging her with being a German spy. (Dad was still in Aruba, fulfilling his contract with the company).

Secretary Hull and the agents reasoned that if a family of German spies wanted to enter the country and do damage, how would they do it without proper papers? They concluded that the family would say that the kid had destroyed the papers.

When they arrested Mom, I guess that in arresting her they figured that they had arrested Mata Hari Sonnenberg.

Even our name of Sonnenberg was suspicious to them. It is both Dutch and German

In arresting Mom—and Dad would be next, the FBI agents said that they were going to put us in an internment camp out west. What would camp life be like? I guess that while incarcerated, I could learn to speak Japanese, raise taro, and construct little rice paper lanterns for American patios and booze fests.

Luckily, people came from Aruba to vouch for us. As a result, the FBI merely confined us to the New York metro area.

***

The arrest incident came back to haunt me many years later when I was in the army. MP's came and took me out of class and escorted me to a general who sat in an immense room behind a desk large enough to host a roller skate derby. I saw that he held a large folder bearing my name.

I saluted.

"At ease. I see you were arrested as a German spy," he said coldly.

"Sir, if you will look at the year that I was arrested and look at my age at the time."

I could see him doing some mental math, and then he laughed. "Return to class," he said.

And now for the history, flawed as it may be. The following details regarding Aruba are based on my aging memories, tales from family and friends, and common knowledge regarding the facts of the island.

Sonnenberg-McGlynn (McGlynn is my Irish stepdad).

ORANJESTAD

A SHORT HISTORY OF ARUBA

Aruba is just fourteen miles off the coast of Venezuela. The island is roughly twenty one miles long and five miles wide. It is a desert, an Arizona dropped into the Caribbean Sea, an island constantly buffeted by twenty knot winds. In fact, the winds are so strong that in the old sailing days, ships could arrive there easily as they were pushed by the prevailing winds. However, returning to their home in Europe was a major undertaking. One passenger even complained after five days of sailing, "The island must be moving too because it is still with us."

As for the discovery of the island, according to the Aruba story, it was around 1499 that Alonzo de Ojeda, a member of Columbus expedition, happened upon the island. He claimed Aruba for Spain by right of discovery, conveniently ignoring the natives who already occupied the nearly barren land.

Apparently the natives did not put up a fuss. I assume that they were ignorant of Western-think which states that if people want to protect their land, they need to put a really big flag at the border and install a public servant to check entry documents. So I guess it serves the natives right that they lost their land. They neglected to put up the official flag to ward off discovery-type predators such as Alonzo who turned their land over to Spain.

As it happened there was nothing worth stealing to enrich Alonzo, and he sailed away to seek his fortune elsewhere in the fashion of the times. He is quoted as saying, "We make money the old-fashioned way. We steal it."

However, in not finding anything of value in Aruba, Alonzo still obtained something of worth. Isabel and Ferdinand granted him the title of *Conquistador*, a great honor which cost the rulers nothing, but the title made Alonzo a hero in those days.

The rulers granting a non-paid honor is an important lesson for all of us. If you make anything a non-paid honor, people will fight over obtaining it.

As for heroes, times have changed and yesterday's hero is now a psycho, homophobe, racist, thief, despoiler of women, a destroyer of nature, a polluter, a testosterone-driven nut-case—oh well, we get the politically correct idea.

Alonzo left and the natives barely noted his departure. But officially the land now belonged to Spain. In fact, Spain sent three Christian missionaries to convert the natives. Evidently, the natives went for the missionaries like kids go for candy. They ate them.

The moral for the Church is, "Never send missionaries to places where food is scarce."

The fate of the Aruba natives is in question. Supposedly, the Spaniards seized them and put them to work in the copper mines of Santo Domingo.

Of course, *seized* is a harsh word and certainly unfair to the Spaniards and what they considered a perfect valid way of life, and who are we to judge them? On the other hand, maybe the Spaniard in charge used a gentler approach and said, "Folks, have we got a deal for you. You have won an all-expense trip to the enchanted isle of Santo Domingo."

Naturally, upon hearing such words, the natives would have eagerly flocked to the ships for their free cruise.

Oh, well, just a thought.

With the natives gone, the island of Aruba had nothing left of use. Therefore, the Spaniards abandoned it.

Not long afterwards, a ship captain either dumped some goats or the goats fell overboard. At any rate, the goats swam to the island.

Having no enemies, they multiplied, which explains the numerous goat descendants roaming around the place today.

Spain was not destined to hold the islands forever, however. In one of those numerous wars that Europeans engaged in, Spain lost the islands to the Dutch, not that the loss mattered much.

According to history, in 1634 the Dutch acquired Aruba, Bonaire, Curacao and some other islands.

To keep the islands, the Dutch sent 300 settlers. I have no idea how the rulers chose the settlers. Were the settlers felons such as the British shipped to Australia? In other words, did the Dutch rulers get rid of tulip thieves, nasty people who spit into the canals, or people who smoked their pipes in non-smoking zones and the like?

But perhaps the Dutch rulers used salesmanship. (Note: *Salesmanship* is a forbidden word in America because it denotes gender).

As for the Dutch salespersonship, it may have gone something like this: "We have a few slots available on a first-come, first-served basis for those who would like free land in the tropical paradise of Aruba. For those chosen, there would be no more fierce Dutch winters in which you would have to get sewn into your underwear to stay warm. No more icicles hanging from your nose. Sign up now. You may be one of the lucky ones chosen!"

At any rate, the islands that the Dutch obtained from Spain fell under Dutch rule with the exception of St. Martin, an island shared with France.

As for St. Martin, according to the story of the split, a Frenchman and a Dutchman started off, back-to-back, and where they met on the opposite side of the island determined the line that would run from where they started to where they finished. The Frenchman walked the fastest, and France controls most of the island today.

Of course, the islands needed a ruler. Therefore, the Dutch installed Peter Stuyvesant as governor. People said that he was harsh, nasty, brutish, nasty, biased, unforgiving, conceited, and rash. The Dutch rulers considered those his good points.

The islanders got rid of Peter in 1647 when the Dutch rulers sent him and his wooden leg off as governor of New Amsterdam. The British attacked and Peter lost the town. New Amsterdam became New York City.

Somehow, it seems unfair to attack a guy with a wooden leg. The Disabilities Act was passed to ensure that such things don't ever happen again.

As for the wooden leg, people are still looking for it. Maybe Hollywood could make another Indiana Jones movie about finding the wooden leg. For excitement, such a film would rank right up there at the top along with finding the Lost Ark, an Ark which I figure is probably resting in some hut in Africa and used to store gourds, the gold having been stripped and sold over 2000 years ago.

As for Peter's wooden leg, my guess is that some housewife, chilled by a harsh New York winter, burned it for its heat.

Meanwhile in Aruba, the people tried farming which worked well in Europe. However, Aruba does not lend itself to farming unless there is a big demand for cactus.

It seems obvious to me that one needs water in order to grow a crop. Aruba doesn't have water to speak of. There is a supposed rainy season from around October to December.

Lacking water, the seeds died in their little graves.

Next, the settlers tried ranching. They forgot that animals also need water. They also need something to eat such as grass. Ranching failed and the settlers were starving.

As a result of all of this misery, the settlers were booking passage back to the Netherlands. However, in 1825, a kid picked up a shiny rock in a gully. The kid had found gold and the Great Aruba Gold Rush was on.

Gold mining lasted until 1908 when mining was no long economically feasible.

GOLD MINING IN ARUBA

Around 1824, a young boy, Willem Rasmijn, while leading his sheep across a dry river bed in Rooi Fluit, picked up a shiny stone. The boy's father sold the stone and went looking for more. The discovery started a great gold rush with hundreds of people rushing to the island in search of their fortune.

However, mining expenses soon outweighed the profits and the gold seekers lost interest. Then in 1867, the London Gold Mining Company built a smelter a Bushirbana near the Natural Bridge. The outfit produced 2075 ounces of gold in the first year of operation

In 1908, the operation ceased. The equipment rusted and the trekinchi (tractor engine) which carried the ore from the island to the smelter was no longer useful. The company abandoned the mill during World War I when dynamite and the raw materials to purify the gold were no longer obtainable.

Photo of the Smelter Ruins at Bushirbana

When the gold ran out, when the food was running out, and when the lack of water made life miserable, once again the Dutch were ready to abandon the island. I can imagine the settlers saying, "Anything to get me outta here. Give me a job checking the Holland dikes for leaks. Even the midnight shift in the dead of winter. I'deven be glad to drive the Zamboni to scrape the ice smooth Tourists know the little Dutch island of Aruba for its luxury hotels, its casinos, and its dazzling beaches.

It's a vacationer's paradise of clear blue skies and never-ending breezes.

However, Aruba has a history beyond luxury hotels and casinos. Tourists might express surprise to discover that the islanders considered abandoning the island. They might express surprise to discover that seven escapees from Devil's Island found their way there—and their eventual fate.

There is also the story of Aruba's part in the sinking of the Antilla just offshore after the Nazis invaded the Netherlands.

Then there is the account of the German U-Boat, the U-156, which accomplished what others thought impossible by reaching Aruba to destroy the refinery, the largest in the world at that time.

Had the attack been successful, the outcome of World War II might have been different because Aruba's refinery produced 95 percent of the high octane fuel needed for airplanes.

Readers will also discover how an island which was almost abandoned became prosperous because an oil tanker from Venezuela's Lake Maracaibo needed a

LIFE IN ARUBA

Almost everyone had animals such as chickens, pigs, and so on. The people kept the animals in the home and allowed them to roam in and out of the house. They animals roamed the unpaved streets and defecated everywhere.

The people cluttered their yards with garbage and other trash because the government did not have a trash collection. The trash had piled up for over 300 years and the mess was awesome.

Water came from water holes, the water thickening into muddy slurry. These muddy water holes became a breeding ground for insects. People sickened from the unsanitary condition of the island.

The place stunk of garbage, sick people, and crap.

Houses had shutters which the people closed during the days against the heat. At night, the people opened the shutters and anything which flew in could fly out. Arubans did not concern themselves with the coming and going of the insects.

The Arubans separated their properties with low walls in the town and with cactus in the country. Cactus not only made a good barrier, but the natives also made soup from it. They also ate iguanas which I am told tastes like chicken.

No grass grew, which meant the natives did not have cows. The lack of cows meant that there was no milk for infants other than a mother's milk.

As for marriage, according to lore—that's my Uncle Clarence. If a couple wished to marry, they notified the families. The families got together to erect a house in the country, leaving the roof off and the couple exposed to the elements. If the couple could still stand each other after two years, the families met again and put a roof on the house.

As for the cities and the color scheme, an 18th Century governor prescribed the order of colors which may be used. Supposedly, he stepped out of his house one day and was blinded momentarily by the glare off of white houses. He passed a law stating that white may not be used—only pastels and in a particular order.

For street lighting, fifteen kerosene lamps lit the dark, and the governor appointed a man to light the lamps each evening.

Civil service and tenure being what it is, I figure that some political supporter is still collecting a salary with health care and pension benefits although the kerosene lights are long gone.

Aruba did not merit a governor—only a lieutenant governor who reported to the governor in Curacao. The lieutenant-governor of Aruba resided in what was known as the Commander's House, the former title of the head of government being commander. The natives referred to him as *Jabass—yes boss.*

Jabass even had an official outfit. He had to wear a dark blue frock coat of cloth or cashmere. The coat had to be lined with blue silk.

The high collar and facings were embroidered with gold and orange branches, two and a half inches wide. The buttons on the coat had to bear the initial W. The buttons were gilt.

Under the frock coat, the commander wore a vest of white cloth. His trousers had to be white with gold lace on the seams.

On his head, the commander wore a tricorne--a three-cornered hat.

Finally, the commander had to carry a gold-hilted sword.

The outfit was official until 1955. The outfit was dumped because emerging rock bands started to wear similar, crazy outfits. That's what happened. I wouldn't lie to you about this, you know.

Furthermore as part of his duties, the commander was obliged to sit at Santa Cruz and Sabaneta every second week to hear complaints and suggestions.

The lieutenant-governor made the rounds on jackass, until around the last of the 1920's, when Lt Governor Wagemaker ordered a Packard from the United States. It was shipped unassembled.

As for looking at the commander who was traveling by jackass while wearing an outfit that members of an American rock band would die for, no one dared to laugh at the crazy scene. We learn early not to laugh at anyone of importance. It's a survival mechanism. We're trained to say, "You look great"—even at the person in the casket.

JAN FREDERICK QUAST

Around 1920, 1921, Queen Wilhelmina of the Netherlands and the officials at The Hague sent Nikolaas Brantjes to Curacao, famous for its rum. She sent Jan Frederick Quast to Aruba, famous for goats, divi-divi pods, and aloe.

Quast was to serve under Governor Brantjes as lieutenant governor.

Quast's salary? The government paid him 2700 gulden a year with another 1800 kicked in to take charge of Aruba.

Arriving in Aruba, Quast found 300 years of garbage and animals in people's homes or roaming free in the streets. There were no street markers or addresses for the homes. The island lacked drinking water. The food source was uneven. The island had no electricity, no paved roads, and no transportation other than horses or jackasses.

Furthermore, Quast had to don the official uniform and ride three hours on a jackass to Santa Cruz and Sabaneta every two weeks to hear citizen complaints. There was no automobile for the lieutenant-governor to make the trip easier.

Clearly, work needed to be done to improve island life.

However, once appointed, Quast did his job as he envisioned it by keeping enormous records in the state ledgers on everything. He recorded the births and deaths of both people and beasts. The birth of a jackass took up space in the books right next to the birth of a child.

Quast also toured every household and examined the housekeeping in each one, recording the names of the people and their offenses. He even cited people whose homes had dirty lamp wicks, filling ledger after ledger with such snore-inducing events.

While Quast filled ledgers, people around the world bought cars, and cars needed gas to run their engines. The gas came from oil, and Lake Maracaibo, Venezuela, had plenty.

In 1925, Quast met with John Eman and Richard Beaujon to discuss a meeting with representatives of Lago Oil of Canada. Afterwards, Quast met with Captain Clark and Mr. Roger.

The reason for the meeting?

Lago needed to dock a tanker and all of the other ports on the other islands were taken Thus Quast gave Lao permission docked a tanker in Port Aruba at San Nicolas. More dockings followed. Next, the company needed storage tanks to handle the oil which the tankers pumped from Lake Maracaibo. So Lago built the storage tanks. More and more ships arrived, more oil, and more storage tanks. Then Lago built the refinery.

The refinery required workers, living quarters, electricity, water, food, a clubhouse, and a hospital. The refinery eventually became the largest refinery in the world, one which made 90 percent of the high octane gas needed for airplanes.

Ships jammed the port going in and out. There was more work than workers. Life on the island became brisk. Money and supplies poured in. Oil left Aruba for Bayonne, New Jersey.

Aruba's economic growth had just passed that of Curacao. Governor Brantjes sent his congratulations to Lieutenant-Governor Quast. Governor Brantjes also made his own arrangements for Curacao to get into the oil business.

By now, Quast was having trouble finding time for both the oil business and his ledgers. Oil company execs figured that the island needed someone more aggressive, someone who was more rough-and-tumble than the bookish Quast to make the necessary improvements.

Therefore, officials at The Hague fired Quast and appointed Isaac Wagemaker as the new lieutenant-governor. The officials made the change without notifying Quast who was out making his household inspection rounds.

The Wagemakers, Isaac age 44 and his wife Fredericka age 41, arrived in Aruba on December 15, 1928.

Hearing of his replacement, an embarrassed Quast rushed to an outgoing ship as secretly as possible. I can imagine him grumbling about ingratitude and a ruined Christmas. After all, he was the one who brought prosperity to Aruba and got dumped as his reward.

Arriving in Oranjestad, the Wagemakers found the Commander's House, the official residence, was a shambles because of Quast's hurried departure. Food still lay on the table, the beds were unmade, and the place was a general mess.

The islanders, who had submitted to eight years of Quast's inspections, reports of dirty wicks and bad housekeeping, gloated and happily shared the story of the messes left at the Commander's House.

Quast 1875-1953 A Final Note

As for former Lieutenant-Governor Quast of Aruba, Queen Wilhelmina just before her abdication on August 23, 1948, offered him the Knighthood of the Nederlandse Leeuw—the Dutch Lion.

He turned down knighthood, saying that the Dutch Lion was the lowest class award and he was declining it.

ISAAC WAGEMAKER

Because of the oil, the new refinery, and the brisk economy, Quast had found himself without a job and humiliated in the process. His replacement, Isaac Wagemaker, became the new lt. governor in 1928.

Isaac Wagemaker settled into the Commander's House and started attacking his duties by starting work on the first map of Oranjestad and its environs. To date, no one had seen any need for maps, People believed that if a person got lost on the small island, they could not be lost for long.

Wagemaker had made careful notes of street names so that he could lay out a rough grid. Then he assigned numbers to each property. He would know, therefore, who owned each property, who was responsible for its condition, who was responsible for its taxes, and to whom the mail would go. Eventually, there would be electric lines and phone lines installed at those properties.

Clearly, Wagemaker was the rough and tumble man the officials had hoped for. He was a man in a hurry. He ate his eggs or whatever his wife could find for food. Then he toured the town, thinking of the necessary changes. He had no time for ledgers, household inspections, and lamp wicks.

He knew the problems. He had seen the animals roaming freely around the yards and the streets. He had seen the waterholes. He had seen the garbage. He had seen that many of the citizens were sick.

Wagemaker issued his first proclamation. "Close the waterholes." He explained that the waterholes bred diseases and made people sick.

The people, given a choice between dirty water and no water, rioted. They wanted water, dirty or not.

"I will get water for you," Wagemaker promised. He hired well drillers. The water they found was unfit to drink.

Then Wagemaker hired a dowser who claimed that there was an underground stream from the mainland to Aruba. The dowser told Wagemaker's workers where to dig. The people gathered to watch. Finally, water burst to the sky, and the people celebrated wildly. The celebration, however, was short-lived. The water was brackish.

The people threatened another riot. They complained that Wagemaker had closed their waterholes, and as a result, they had no water. At least, Quast had not closed their waterholes, they said, and Quast had not disturbed their routines.

"Open the waterholes or we riot," they said.

Luckily, Wagemaker avoided the riot. He had had the foresight to request water from Standard Oil, the new owner of Lago. Evan at the moment, ships loaded with water from the Hudson River in New York sat at the docks.

"Take your containers and go to the docks for fresh water," Wagemaker said.

Afterwards, lining up on the docks became another routine, a social one, during which people exchanged the gossip as they waited to fill their five gallon jugs.

The solution was a pleasant one for the officials at Lago because once the oil was pumped out of the ships in Bayonne, the ships risked riding too high. The water taken from the Hudson River supplied stability for the trip back to the island.

While the people lined up regularly at the docks for their fresh water, Wagemaker started the construction of a water de-salinization plant to remove the salt from the sea water.

However, the people complained about the taste of the distilled water. It didn't have any. Chemists solved the problem by adding mud to make it tasty—the chemists simply did not tell the people about the mud.

With the water problem solved, Wagemaker made his second proclamation: "Anyone within city limits must dispose of all farm-type animals. Your chickens and pigs have to go within the week, or else."

Wagemaker told the people that either they got rid of the animals or the government would seize the animals and slaughter them. There would be no more herds of animals roaming the streets, especially pigs who can be vicious. More people in Aruba had been injured in bouts with pigs than from falling off horses.

There would be no more animals sleeping in the houses.

Once again, the people threatened to riot. How dare the commander interfere with their rights! But they wondered if Wagemaker would really seize their animals and slaughter them. Would he really do it?

From what the people had seen of him and his rough manner, they concluded that he would do exactly as he had threatened.

Clearly, the people did not realize that animals defecating in the streets led to disease. They did not realize that chickens give Cryptococcosis which starts as a fever, and there were plenty of people with fevers on the island.

Then the people develop hacking coughs from the disease, a cough so fierce that people clutch their chests and their stomachs to prevent their lungs from popping out through their mouths. The people gasp for air. Their muscles hurt. They think that their hearts are going to give out. They lose weight.

Then they eat chicken soup to ease the pain of the illness.

Then while the people are dealing with diseases from chickens, they also had to deal with diseases from pigs. Pigs carry trichinosis. It is a disease in which a worm hooks onto a person's intestines.

"Your animals are making you sick," the lt. Governor said. "They are killing you."

"But they are our animals."

"If I find them at the end of the week, I will kill them."

By the end of the week, all of the animals had new homes in the countryside, or they had been slaughtered.

Having been threatened too often with rioting, Wagemaker tried a new tactic for his next project: The 300 years of rotting garbage.

The Lt. Governor sent handbills which told the citizens to pile all of their accumulated garbage at the street on such-and-such a date. He also enlisted the aid of the priests who said to the congregations, "God is tired of looking at dirty messes of your garbage, and He is nauseated breathing its foul odors. Clean it up and put your garbage at the street for pickup."

This time, there was no rioting. The people gathered the garbage, the broken furniture, the rusted pails, broken pottery, and animal bones and so on and placed the accumulation at the street.

The first garbage collection took over three weeks to complete. Wagemaker had to work out routes because the three trucks were criss-crossing. They were duplicating each other's routes. At times, the drivers got into fights over collecting the garbage when they all arrived simultaneously at a house.

Some citizens complained that they had waited over three weeks and the trucks still had not made a pickup.

Then one truck broke down and emptied its load on the street. People, thinking that the pile represented a new dump site, added to it.

While all of this confusion was going on, Wagemaker received complaints that the collections crews were dumping the garbage everywhere. To correct the situation, the Lt. Governor ordered the three trucks to retrieve the garbage that had been dumped in gullies, in the countryside, on the beaches, and on the dunes.

Wagemaker scolded himself. "I forgot to tell the collection crews what to do with the trash." He thought about the problem for a few minutes and then he issued an order. "Take it to the north side of the island past the Natural Bridge and throw it into the ocean."

The north side of the island is rough. It is jagged. The wind-driven sea is wild. The place is of no use for swimming or anything else.

The men tossed the trash into the sea. The sharks and the barracudas fought over it.

Having established a safe water system, having cleared the towns of farm animals in the streets, and having rid the country of the unsanitary garbage, Wagemaker next turned his attention to transportation.

His transportation.

He had no intention of making the ungainly rounds every two weeks on a jackass as his predecessor had done. There would be no trip for him in his official uniform and tricorne hat while his arms flapped in the air, and as the beast bit and passed wind.

Although jackasses symbolize humility, and their riders appear humble, Wagemaker decided that real people ignore humble people. Humble people can be ignored. Humble people could starve and die and no one would notice. Humble people speak, and no one listens.

Wagemaker thought that something symbolizing authority would be a better choice. Therefore, he ordered a Packard, a world-recognized symbol.

The car arrived by ship. It was unassembled.

Wagemaker asked for help from anyone who knew how to use a screwdriver or a wrench.

It was a men only project, of course, because according to Western culture all men are born with a mechanical gene which allows them to understand the workings of every gadget in the world—or kick it if they don't.

To compensate for men's mechanical gift, they are deprived of verbal ability, sensitivity, and shopping genes.

Bit by bit the car took shape until it stood proudly as a completed Packard. Everyone celebrated in the usual Aruba fashion. They drank. Drinking, they thought was healthy. "Throw a worm into a glass of rum and see what happens. The worms dies. So drink and you will never have worms."

"How about ordering an airplane?" the crew said.

Wagemaker declined tactfully.

Next, the Lt. Governor turned his attention to paving the roads: Oost Street, Noord, Klip, Heren, and Nassau. Then he ordered a bridge over the Spanish Lagoon where pirate ships used to set in for repairs. The bridge made sense because it would save driving time between Oranjestad and San Nicolas—and Lago Oil.

Wagemaker, wearing his official uniform of tricorne hat, blue frock coat, white vests and white trousers, opened the completed bridge on September 26, 1929.

The islanders had seldom seen such magnificence. The bridge was a marvel. Wagemaker was a marvel. The days was as crystalline as blue sapphires. It was a day for an exaltation of larks—if larks could withstand the scorching sun. A parrot sat on a bush and searched beneath its wings for bugs to eat. Lizards darted across the sand. The band struck up the chords of the national anthem, the *Willemus.* It was the occasion of the year.

The bridge sank six months later.

The Lt. Governor's next project was an unexpected one.

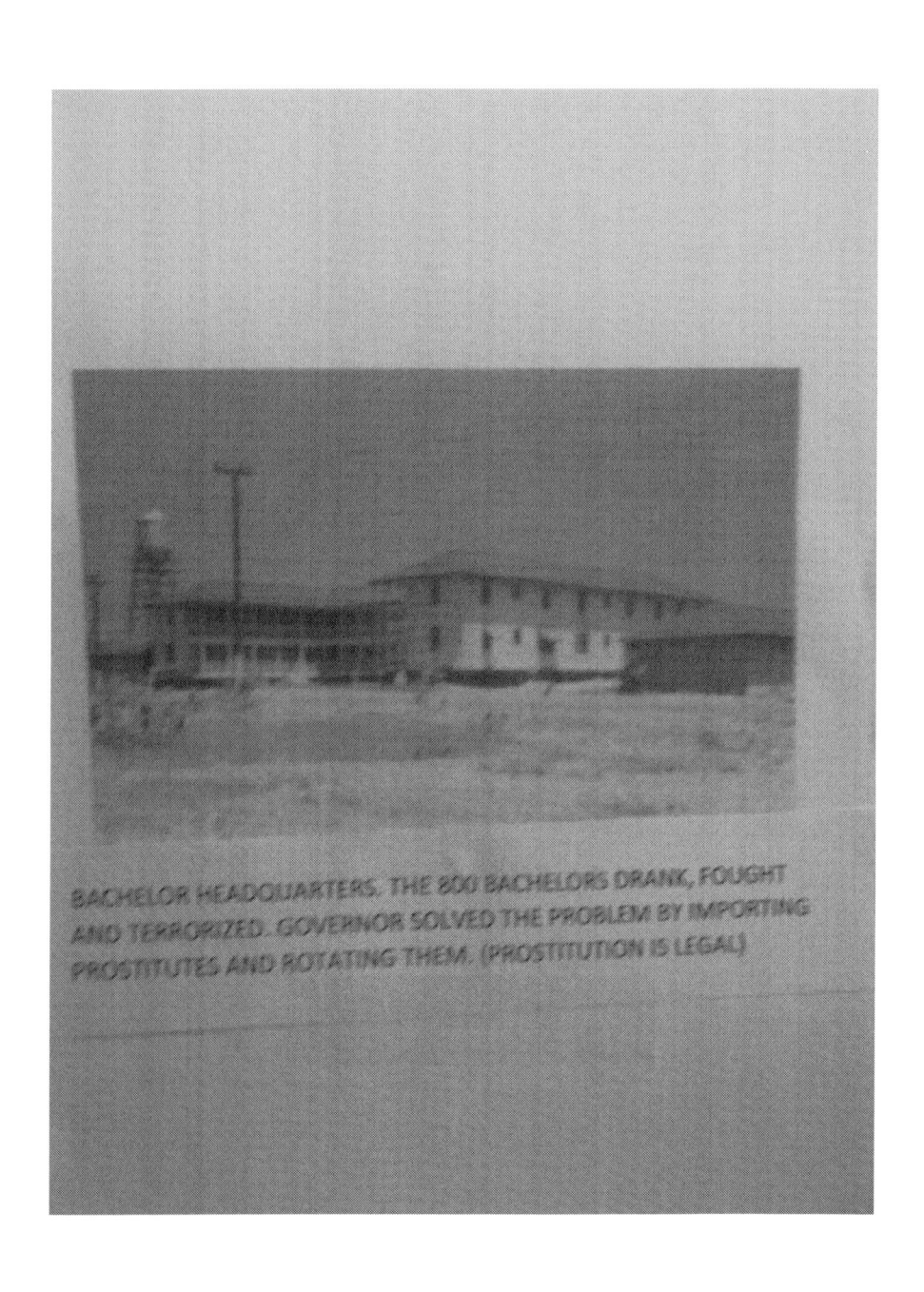

BACHELOR HEADQUARTERS. THE 800 BACHELORS DRANK, FOUGHT AND TERRORIZED. GOVERNOR SOLVED THE PROBLEM BY IMPORTING PROSTITUTES AND ROTATING THEM. (PROSTITUTION IS LEGAL)

THE BACHELORS, THE COPS, AND THE RIOT OF 1929

Bachelor Headquarters. The 800 bachelors drank, fought, and terrorized. The Lt. Governor attempted to solve the problem by importing prostitutes. (Prostitution was legal)

The oil refinery, then the largest in the world, needed lots of workers. The company supplied homes for the families, but for the bachelors, they built a huge apartment barracks.

The bachelors gave new meaning to the word party. Of course, hot sun, cheap drinks, and a steady, well-paying job are a winning combination for bachelors anywhere in the world. Having little to do except drink, the bachelors fought in the barracks. They fought in the streets. They caroused into late hours.

The bachelors drank to forget. They drank for courage. They drank to laugh. They drank because they were sad. They fought over offenses that they could not remember. They nursed black eyes, cut lips, bruised bones and broken teeth.

Most of the fights occurred on the tenth of the month. The tenth was payday for whites Payday for Blacks came every two weeks because Lago did not believe that Blacks knew how to budget their money to last all month. And the company paid in gold because the Chinese workers refused to work for paper.

The citizens complained to Wagemaker. The carousing was keeping them awake. In contrast to the bachelors who stayed up until all hours, the islanders ate around 7:30 and went to bed by 10:00.

The islanders complained as Wagemaker tried to come up with a solution, and he found one that he thought would be beneficial to all: Prostitution.

Wagemaker sent for ten prostitutes. The government set them up in San Nicolas and to insure safety, inspected them for diseases regularly. Ten women, therefore, had the task of taking care of 800 men. On payday, the tenth of every month, the whites lined up outside the bordello. On the week before the tenth and the week after, the blacks lined up at the bordellos.

"I can't understand it," Wagemaker said. "The Whites who refuse to share a bench, a drinking fountain, or a restaurant with Blacks, will share prostitutes with them."

The prostitutes stayed in Aruba for two month before exchanging places with their co-workers in Venezuela. Thus, there were new girls every two month.

However, the problem continued.

One can never underestimate the amount of mischief that 800 bachelors can do when thrown together. The bachelors had many hours of leisure time for mischief. They had nothing to do because Aruba really did not have any entertainment to speak of. Therefore, the 800 entertained themselves with drunken brawls, horseplay, practical jokes, and carousing until all hours of the night and making a nuisance of themselves by urinating in public.

There had never been any crime in 300 years. There were no cops and no jail.

Wagemaker advertised for a police force. Nobody on Aruba applied. Nobody in the Netherlands applied. Therefore, the lt. Governor advertised in Dutch Guiana (now Surinam).

Twenty six men answered the ad. They had no experience and they were black. All they knew of police work were the beatings the police in Paramaribo had given them.

Wagemaker issued the men uniforms and billy clubs. He told them to stop the rowdy behavior on the island. Their pay? Twenty six gulden a month--$13.50. He also offered them $50 for each person arrested.

With such a reward, the police traveled in gangs and arrested with enthusiasm. They stopped and clubbed the bachelors. They arrested American sailors off the ship, took the sailors' possession, and threw the sailors into jail, an act which forced the sailors' captain to come for them and to pay a ransom.

Then the police clubbed and American sailor to death. Other men were beaten bloody by the cops. In what became known as the Riot of 1929, over 300 men, outraged and objecting to the actions of the cops, marched through the streets of San Nicolas and attacked the police gangs, beating, them breaking arms and legs, and knocking out their teeth. Then they threw the policemen into their own jail, placed dynamite around it, and threatened to blow it up with the cops still inside. "Get rid of these cops," the mob yelled, "or we will blow them all to kingdom come!"

Wagemaker fired the cops and wrote to Queen Wilhelmina, asking for help. The queen sent forty men from the Netherlands to enforce the laws. Several of the 300 plus men were arrested. My grandfather, Edwin Harris was among those jailed. After a trial, he was freed.

THE DEVIL'S ISLAND ESCAPEES: ARRIVAL IN ARUBA IN 1937

In 1937, seven escapees from Devil's Island arrived in Aruba after a thousand mile trip in an open sailboat. The men were dehydrated and suffering from massive sunburns, their skin cracked and peeling.

Lt. Governor Wagemaker sent the men to the barren north shore to hide them and to allow a chance for them to heal. They threw up the first food that they tried to eat. Their tongues were swollen and their eyes puffed. They screamed in pain when they opened their mouths.

Wagemaker hoped that the men would recover quickly because the French had already landed in the nearby island of Curacao and were searching for the escapees.

Three tense weeks passed. Wagemaker provisioned a small boat and told the men to sail west to Colombia immediately if they valued their freedom. "You will be safe in Colombia," he told them. "The French do not have an extradition treaty with Colombia."

At the same time that the men were leaving Port Aruba, 160 French marines landed in Oranjestad and were going door to door in their search, their invasion clearly a violation of international law.

What did people do while the French were taking over the island? They did as they always did. They went to work. They shopped. They visited friends. The cops continued to direct traffic.

The escapees reached Columbia, hid their boat, and waded upstream where the citizens greeted them wildly. The people gave them a huge celebration and got them drunk.

The following morning, French marines from the Primoguet surrounded the men and hauled them back to Devil's Island.

The men would not be among the 27 men out of 70,000 men who never escaped Devils' Island and remained free. (Photos are from our family album)

Devil's Island Escapees. Photos from the family album.

GERMANY INVADES THE NETHERLANDS

Germany's Von Ribbentrop invented the pre-emptive strike excuse by stating that German was invading the Netherlands to protect that country's neutrality.

Queen Wilhelmina of the Netherlands issued a statement: I herewith direct a flaming protest against this unprecedented violation of good faith. I and my government now will do our duty."

Wilhelmina, born August 31, 1880, was almost sixty when the Germans attacked. It certainly was not a good time for someone her age to rush to English asylum from her home to escape the Germans.

However, the queen was a sturdy, no-nonsense lady who read her Bible every day. She planned everything to the smallest detail and allowed no laughter or frivolity. She always wore practical Dutch clothes. Her daughter Juliana complained about the severe nature of her mother and the frugalities. The palace, Hui ten Bosch, was always cold, the lights always shut off, and Juliana was forced to wear long underwear to keep warm.

The Germans who attacked the Netherlands were especially anxious to seize the queen to lend an air of legitimacy to their authority.

It must have been a terrible night for the family as they tried to make their way to safety in the back of an armored truck to the North Sea where a British ship waited.

Four days later on May 14, 1940, General Winkelmann surrendered the Netherlands to the Germans.

ARUBA AT WAR, MAY 10, 1940

"I and my government now will do our duty," Queen Wilhelmina said. As a member of the government, Lt. Governor Wagemaker regarded the queen's statement as an order. It meant that he must attack the German whenever and wherever he found them. In this case, according to orders, he decided to attack the German ship, the *Antilla* which lay about 1000 yards offshore from the California Lighthouse at the western tip of Aruba.

When Germany invaded Poland in 1939, the Allies ordered the blockade of all German shipping, the *Antilla* had recently come from Galveston Texas, with a cargo of sulfur scheduled for Europe. Trapped by the war, Captain Schmidt and the newly built ship sought refuge ofF the coast of neutral Netherlands colony, Aruba.

The captain tried several times to escape, but Allied warships lay just outside the three mile limit, waiting to capture the ship.

When the Germans invaded the Netherlands under the pretext of saving the neutral country from a British-French invasion. The Dutch government issued orders that all German ships should be seized immediately and the crews arrested.

Governor Wagemaker, according to the story which most like other stories may be embellished so that it is no longer recognizable, sent the marines who were armed with rifles last fired around 1900. For the marines, he issued the entire supply of the island's ammunition: eighty bullets.

The group sailed to where the Antilla lay at anchor, just off Malmok, and called for Captain Schmidt, who came to the rail. "What do you want?"

"We want to come aboard. We want you to surrender the ship."

I think that Captain Schmidt told them in reply something like "Go pound sand."

At any rate, he refused to lower the gangplank. This exchange continued for a half hour until the group saw an inky smoke rising from the *Antilla*. The ship was on fire.

The captain had delayed while his men were setting fire to the ship and scuttling it to keep it from falling into enemy hands.

When the ship was well ablaze, the captain ordered his men to abandon ship. Thirty five crew members leaped into the sea and swam towards the California lighthouse—or the Dutch marines took them by launch to the island, according whichever story is correct.

The *Antilla* rolled over on its side, its masts sticking above the water, the masts pointing in the direction of the island. As for the shipwreck, it is still where it sank on May 10, 1940. It is now a tourist attraction.

THE ANTILLA, TRAPPED OFFSHORE BY WWII. CAPT SCHMIDT SET IT AFIRE AND SCUTTLED IT MAY 10, 1940. THE 35 CREW MEMBERS SWAM ASHORE AND SET UP CAMP.

Germans from the Antilla-May 10, 1940

After the German captain had ordered his men to set fire to the Antilla, and after the men opened the sea valves to scuttle the ship, the captain ordered the 35 men to abandon ship. The Dutch lieutenant-governor (Wagemaker) must have been very surprised seeing the men leaping into the sea.

The Germans swam to the California lighthouse and set up camp. the photo shows one of them in a crude shelter, called mockingly enough the Schloss Heidelberg-Castle Heidelberg.

This is the hut that the German crew built after they swam ashore from the Antilla. The men disappeared one by one.

When we were in Aruba in 1970, we took a boat to see the wreckage, which sticks up slightly in the water. The guide said, "It is just some ship which went down." He had no idea of what had happened.

The next morning, May 11, 1940, the French ship, the *Primauget* docked off Oranjestad and disgorged 180 French marines.

"The Germans are bombing Rotterdam," the French captain said. "It is only days until your General Winkelmann surrenders and your government falls. We are here to protect you. The gasoline you produce must not fall into the hands of the Germans."

"We will do what we can to help," Wagemaker said.

"What can you do against the Germans?" The Frenchman seemed amused. "France has the best outfitted, the largest army and navy in the world. We are unbeatable."

France lasted against the Germans for about a month.

While the *Primoguet* stood at anchor in Oranjestad, German columns entered France through Sudan and raced to the English Channel, cutting off Flanders and trapping the Allied forces at Dunkirk.

The British, sailing anything which floated, rescued the Allied forces trapped at Dunkirk in one of the greatest escapes in history.

On June 13, 1940, the Germans entered Paris, and the French withdrew their troops from Aruba, leaving the refinery defenseless.

Lago sent notices to its people that in the event of bombing they should hide under a heavy object such as a dining room table.

For their part, the Islanders were relieved that the island was so far from Europe. German planes could not fly such a great distance, and submarines did not have enough range to reach Aruba.

However, the U-boats could reach the eastern United States and the eastern Caribbean. As a result, shipping losses were tremendous.

The United States had no anti-sub ability except one 165 long Coast Guard cutter. The cutter had a top speed of 16 knots; the German subs could easily outrun the cutter.

As for tactics, the German stayed below the surface during the day and raided at night when they could easily spot the tankers against the horizon. A favorite German trick was to surface in a group of ships and sink them using only the deck cannon.

And many of those shipping losses were due to a man on the island who radioed shipping information to the German subs. The man was a Lago company doctor.

In the meantime, the British convoy system had nearly stopped the ship sinkings in the British defense area. Although British officials place the information in the hands of the Americans, officials in Washington chose to ignore it.

The New York Times noted that in the seven months between January 1942 and July 1942, the Germans sank 519 ships in the American defense zone. The British lost only 49.

In Germany, Admiral Doenitz had decided to test the American waters of the Gulf after the development of larger U-Boats. Although the islanders didn't know it, Aruba was within range— with a few alterations to the subs enabling them to carry extra diesel fuel and ammunition.

THE MEN OF THE U-BOATS

German officials in charge of finding volunteers for the U-Boats advertised for volunteers of a special sort. The ads told the men that Germany was looking for men with a special breed of courage.

The ads noted that almost no one had the qualifications to apply for U-boat service.

The ads explained that joining the crew of a U-boat was a great honor. It would be a great adventure, one which might even cost those who were chosen their lives. Almost no one, the ads said, only the special few would be able to withstand the harsh training.

"Membership in the Korps is restricted. We don't take just anybody. Only the best may apply."

It was a clever challenge.

Naturally, after hearing such a challenge, young men flooded the department with requests to join. They asked friends with influence to put in a good word for them. They begged. They cajoled.

They celebrated when the U-Boat Korps admitted them.

Young men, whose mothers bundled them up with the least chill in the weather, found themselves doing calisthenics nearly naked in the snow.

The submariners learned that life aboard a 500 ton U-Boat was cramped and smelly with fifty men crammed into the close quarters. There were on two toilets. Nothing ever dried and the food got moldy. The crew developed rashes. Bathing conditions did not exist, and the sub smelled of sweat and diesel, a smell that did not wear off the sailors even after a week ashore.

The German propaganda machine was already making the men famous. The men had just sunk over 100,000 tons of Allied shipping. They were heroes.

The subs sank so many ships that American military policemen had to round up the tanker captains and force them to their ships. Many times the ships got only a few thousand yards offshore before the Germans sank them.

(My stepfather, McGlynn, a member of the Coast Guard stationed in Puerto Rico, was one of those who had to round up the captains. "I really felt bad about it," he said, "because lots of times the ships would barely get out of port when I saw the explosions."—Later in North Africa he had to check the ID's of those entering the ill-repute houses. British and Canadians could avail themselves of the services, but not Americans).

The U-Boats sank so many tankers that the oil which leaked from their holds blanketed the beaches from Florida to Maine.

Tankers which formerly returned to Aruba with fresh water and food supplies, lay on the continental shelf. Newspapers suppressed all information of the seriousness of the situation for fear of panicking people. Yet, the islanders realized that food and water supplies were low.

WEST INDIES ISLE SHELLED BY SUBMARINES U-156 AND CAPT. HARTENSTEIN ATTACK ARUBA, FEBRUARY 16, 1942.

Aruba, home to the largest refinery in the world at the time, produced 90 percent of the high grade gasoline needed for allied airplanes. The Germans calculated that they could end the war quickly and in their favor if they destroyed the Aruba refinery. The allied war effort would collapse with the destruction of the Lago Refinery in San Nicolas.

The storage tanks and the refinery were at the water's edge. In spite of the vulnerable position, the allies thought that the ocean trip by U-boat impossible. The U-boats had sunk millions of tons of shipping all the way from Florida to New England, but Aruba, off the coast of Venezuela, was beyond their range, the military experts thought.

However, with re-fitting and by adding extra fuel tanks, the U-156 slipped into the Caribbean and at 1:31 in the morning of February

16, 1942, attacked the *Pedernales* and the Oranjestad with torpedoes. The ships exploded and sank in about 230 feet of water. *The Pedernales*, loaded with oil, burst into flames. Fifteen of the twenty two man crew died.

At 3:13, the U-156 torpedoed the *Arkansas* which sank partially. Capt. Hartenstein ordered his men to the deck guns to prepare for attack on the storage tanks. One of the crew neglected to remove the water cap from the 105 mm gun, so when the captain ordered the men to fire, the gun exploded. One man lost his foot. The other man died shortly afterwards of his wounds. The captain ordered the 37 mm flak gun to continue the attack. Although the crew fired 16 rounds, the shells did not pierce the tanks. Hartenstein ordered a cease-fire and set his course for the other end of the island.

THE ATTACK AS NOTED ONSHORE

At one thirty in the morning of February 16, 1942, in a guest house built by Lago Oil, Lt. General Frank Andrews slept the sleep of one who has filled a day with too many duties. On the morning of the fifteenth, he had inspected the defenses on Curacao, intending to stay the night. However, at the last minute, he changed his mind and flew to Aruba. US troops had arrived there five days earlier— February 11, 1942.

After all, the largest refinery in the world needed protection, especially because the refinery produced the highest grade of aviation fuel so vital to the allied war effort.

Lt. General Frank Andrews moved into the guest house which was always kept ready in case of visiting VIP's. The house sat on a small rise overlooking San Nicolas Bay where the company's tankers entered and left. The waters were beautiful, but they were also barracuda-packed. Whalers dumped their refuse there, making the bay a favorite feeding spot for the predators.

Captain Robert Bruskin, Press Relations, and official news photographers Herbert white and William Gerecke, moved in with the general.

Around 1:30 in the morning, a tremendous flash and a violent explosion threw the general out of bed. Night turned into day as the thunderous, deafening explosion lit the sky.

One of the shallow draft tankers had split in two, and thousands of gallons of oil spread quickly across the water. A tower of fire arose from the stricken tanker, the fire spreading quickly until the entire bay was aflame.

Bullets whizzed past the general. "Down!" he yelled. The men lay helplessly on the floor as the tracers flew overhead. The general heard the metallic ring as the bullets hit the storage tanks. He heard the screams of the men in the water. "They are being burned to death. The barracuda are tearing the men apart."

Another explosion shook the port. Another ship went up. The sub had struck again. More oil spilled into the bay and ignited. The general described the height of the inferno as being as high as a mountain. The heat was intense.

The screams continued as the crews of the ships were being torn apart by the barracudas and being to death.

One by one the screams ceased until they were no more.

Shortly afterwards, cars lined the beach, headlights aimed at the bay. The islanders had driven to see what was going on. Then bullets shot out the lights.

The following morning brought stories of a bullet going over the bed of a sleeping woman. She was unharmed. There was a hole in the back of the clubhouse. A large torpedo was found on the beach. The captain had tried to torpedo a storage tank, but the torpedo fell short.

While examining the torpedo, four Dutch marines were killed when the torpedo exploded.

Then the rumors started. It was an entire wolf pack of German subs which had attacked. Germans had landed and they were taking over the streets in the town. The Germans had captured Lt. Governor Wagemaker. The wolf pack was sailing to Panama to blow up the Canal and the waters of the Pacific which were higher than the waters in the gulf would soon flood everything. Aruba would be under water.

People sat under their dining room tables with their family Bibles and prayed.

Why were so many tankers sunk?

It seems that although Wagemaker tried to wake the radio operator shortly after one thirty to warn the other tankers not to come in, the operator refused to get up. Finally, the operator was taken at gunpoint and he radioed other ships not to come in.

As a result of the operator's refusal to get up and go to work, the sub sank nine tankers.

In contrast to the actual damage, National Geographic in the February 1943 issue, wrote that no damage had occurred and no ships sunk.

Although Capt. Hartenstein sank the Pedernales, it was repaired and sailed again. In fact, it took part in the Allied invasion of North Africa.

As for the captain, although the U156 was sunk a few months later, the captain survived. While in the South Atlantic, the U-156 sank a British ship, the *Laconia*, a ship packed with Italian war prisoners and women and children. Realizing the mistake, he captain picked up the people, but there was not enough room in the sub, so he put the survivors atop on deck, meaning that he had to travel above water in the open. While sailing, the Allies spotted the German sub with survivors on deck. The Allies attacked the sub. Because of this, Admiral Doenitz in Germany ordered that in the future no German sub should stop to pick up survivors.

After the war, Hartenstein visited Aruba and apologized for his attack on the island.

The Pedernales. The ships was floated again, supposedly serving in the invasion of North Africa. It was re-floated but certainly never made it to North Africa.

THE END OF THE U-BOATS

The United States soon covered all the gaps in defenses with escort vessels for convoys and small aircraft carriers whose planes left the subs no place to hide.

Bombs, depth charges, shelling, and ramming damaged the subs which then sank by the stern. To right the ships and bring it back to trim, the captain would order the men to run forward while the engines worked at full speed. The pumps also worked at full speed. Often in spite of the captain's and the crew's efforts, the injured sub continued to sink by the stern taking it to greater depths than it was designed for.

Under these conditions, the captain had one last resort. He had to use the last sixty pounds of compressed air to force the sub to surface. Lacking the sixty pounds, the ship went to the bottom.

Sometimes in the captain's haste to surface the sub, releasing the compressed air caused the ship to pop above the waves like a child's bathtub toy.

The hunters had become the hunted.

What must it have been like to serve on a sub under attack?

A US plane drops a bomb on a sub. The sub shakes and the lights flicker. Hundreds of gallons of water pour in. The crew's fears mix with the smell of sweat and diesel fuel.

"Full ahead," the captain orders, hoping that the increased speed will lift the stern. However, even at full speed on both electric motors, the stern continues to sink under the increasing weight of the water pouring in.

"Forward!" the captain yells. He hopes the weight of the men will bring the ship back to trim.

Depth charges explode as four men work the pumps. The stern crackles as the ship descends. The ship loses speed, making the situation even more critical.

Accordingly, the captain orders the air fed and the tanks blown. The sub rises quickly to the surface just in time to see a US destroyer bearing down on them.

There is a deafening crunch as the destroyer rams the sub just aft of the conning tower. Within thirty seconds, the sub sinks beneath the waves taking with it the crew.

THE WRAP-UP

On June 6, 1944, the allies landed in France at Normandy. It marked the beginning of the end for the Germans.

In April 1945, Hitler committed suicide in his Berlin bunker, and Admiral Doenitz became head of the government.

On May 7, 1945, the Germans signed the peace treaty in Rheims. On May 8 it was ratified. Admiral Doenitz was tried at Nuremberg and sentenced to ten years in Spandau. Goering and most of the others were sentenced to hang.

In Aruba, Lieutenant-Governor Wagemaker retired. He had governed the island from 1928 until 1945.

The island had come a long way from the days of earning money with the pods of the divi-divi sold in Hamburg for tanning leather goods.

It was the refinery which changed things.

However, Standard Oil shut down the aging, obsolete refinery in 1985. (Valero, seeing possibilities, has taken it over).

As for the infamous U-156 which attacked the island, after sinking over 22 ships in its 18 months of service, it went down on March 8, 1943, at 12-38 degrees north and 54-39 degrees west, an area of the Atlantic roughly 300 miles east of Martinique. It sank in waters over 3000 feet deep. Captain Hartenstein was its last commander. He survived.

As for the royal family, Queen Wilhelmina returned to the Nooreinde Palace, and Princess Juliana and Bernhard moved into Soestdijk Palace, with Bernhard expressing his anger at having to pay rent to his Mother-in-Law Wilhelmina.

ARUBA MISCELLANEOUS --AT THAT TIME

THE STATE DOES NOT RECOGNIZE CHURCH MARRIAGES. The church does not recognize state marriages. For a marriage to be legal, couple must have two ceremonies.

ARUBA HAD NO CHILDHOOD DISEASES. When I came to the USA, I had no immunity to anything. Measles, chickenpox, mumps, colds etc followed almost immediately.

BOYS GET SMALLPOX VACCINATIONS ON LEFT ARM. (A GUY MUST BE RIGHT-HANDED)

GIRLS ARE VACCINATED ON THE FOOT SO THAT HER BEAUTY IS NOT SPOILED WITH A SCAR.

SCHOOLS AT THE TIME WENT ONLY TO THE 8TH GRADE.

WOMEN MAY NOT WEAR SLACKS. (THAT'S MEN'S CLOTHING). No bare shoulders or bare midriffs. Woman could wear only dresses or skirts.

MEN COULD NOT APPEAR AT THE BEACH BARE-CHESTED.

STORES CLOSED AT NOON EVERY DAY FOR A TWO HOUR BREAK.

SEATS ARE ASSIGNED IN CHURCH AND PAID FOR ON A YEARLY BASIS.

CURRENCY:

GULDEN. RATE OF EXCHANGE—ONE GULDEN EQUALS FIFTY CENTS IN USA MONEY.

PAPIAMENTO IS THE LANGUAGE: The Spanish influence is obvious, but there is a bit of Dutch lingo. (House may be *cas or kas* from the Spanish *casa*).

Verbs do not change. 'ta' stands for I am, you are and he is, etc

I am -mi ta. To say "I was-Mi a ta. "a' makes it past tense. I will be-Mi lo ta . "lo" makes it future.

I have=Mi tin. Mi a tin—I had Mi lo tin-I will have

A SHORT EXAMPLE OF THE LANGUAGE:

Bon bini-welcome	homber-man
Bon dia-good day,	muher-woman
Bon tarde-good afternoon	mener di skol-teacher

Bon nochi-goodnight.	kantante-singer
Bon noche-good night	bailado-dancer
Danki-thanks	Mi tin un buki-I have a book
Por fabor-please	E tin un pushi-She has a cat.
Si-yes, no-no	Nos tin un kacho. We have a dog.
Goodbye-ayo	Kiko bo number ta? What's your name?
Studiante-student	

A FINAL NOTE

Aruba today is a wonderful place of dazzling, white sandy beaches; huge posh hotels; scuba diving; and a vibrant night life.

However, that is not the Aruba I left so many years ago while World War II raged.

After the war, the oil company offered my Dad a job in the Dutch East Indies. Dad thought about it, and luckily he turned it down. As it turned out, we missed being there for the revolution, the revolution which created the nation known as Indonesia. I don't regret missing a revolution.

The information in this short history is based on an accumulation of notes that I made more than forty years ago, notes of stories from grandparents, parents, uncles, aunts, Godparents, and their friends. Some is common knowledge or from news items at the times. It is not meant to be scholarly.

Roger, who was instrumental in obtaining permission from Lt. Governor Quast to dock a tanker at Port Aruba, signed the English copy of my birth certificate (as British ambassador to Aruba).

The photos are copies of photos in the family album, photos such as the ones of the Devil's Island escapees, the hut built by the crew of the sunken *Antilla* and so on. Some of the photos photos are at least 80 years old.

There are some more recent photos taken when I took my children to the island for a visit. My children loved it; I felt out of place. As it is said, "The past is another country. We don't live there anymore."

I prepared this work at the request of my children. I prepared it for them, for my four grandchildren, and for my five great grandchildren.

Because of the hearsay, gossipy type of accounts, there are certainly errors for which I apologize.

One last photo regarding the beating death of a US sailor and the 1929 riot which followed.

The photo below shows the *USS Omaha* in Port Aruba. Note the seaplane which the ship carries port side.

The photo on the bottom shows US sailors dressed for liberty in Aruba.

The sailors were easy targets for the cops which Lt. Governor Wagemaker had hired to keep the peace. Unfortunately, Wagemaker also offered the cops a bonus for each person arrested.

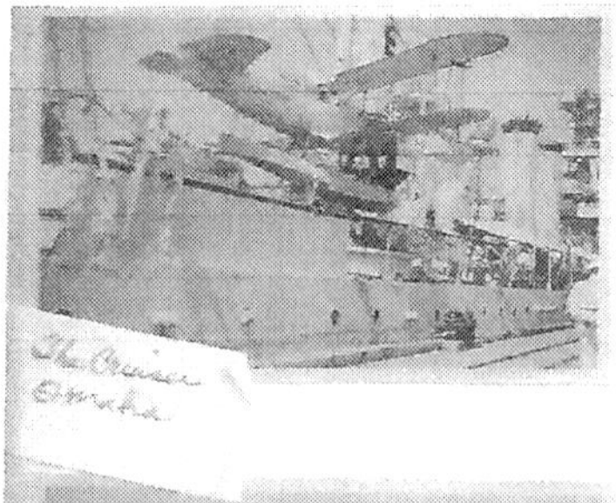
The Cruiser
Omaha

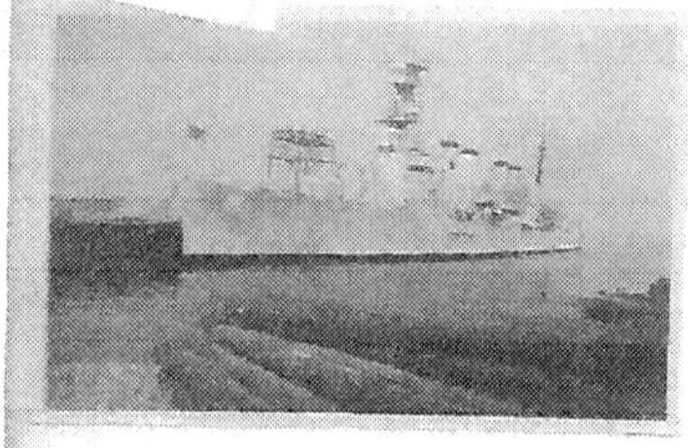

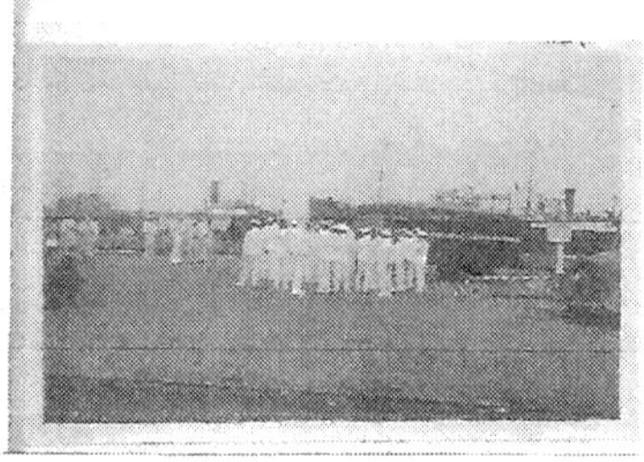

DIVI-DIVI TREE. THE CONSTANT 20 KNOT WINDS FROM THE NORTHEAST SHAPE THE TREES

Aruba today

Printed in Great Britain
by Amazon